AMERICA FOR FREE WORKING MEN !

Mechanics, Farmers and Laborers

READ !

HOW SLAVERY INJURES THE FREE WORKING MAN.

THE SLAVE-LABOR SYSTEM

THE

FREE WORKING-MAN'S WORST ENEMY.

By CHARLES NORDHOFF.

NEW YORK:

HARPER & BROTHERS, PUBLISHERS, FRANKLIN SQUARE.

1865.

PARTS OF THIS PAMPHLET HAVE APPEARED IN THE EDITORIAL
COLUMNS OF THE NEW YORK "EVENING POST."

CONTENTS.

What Democratic Leaders think of Slavery,

"Speaking for myself, slavery is to me the most repugnant of all human institutions. No man alive should hold me in slavery; and if it is my business no man, with my consent, shall hold another. Thus I voted in 1851, in Ohio, with my party, which made the new constitution of my own State. I have never defended slavery; nor has my party."

Speech of Hon. S. S. Cox, of Ohio, in the House of Representatives, Jan. 12, 1865.

Mr. Brooks, of New York, in defending slavery, "did not pretend to speak for the democratic party. Indeed, he does not profess to speak for it, but rather as an old line Whig, having now his views independent of all machines of party. During the last session he held that slavery was dead. Gentlemen should not object to his eulogizing the deceased, but by so doing he does not intend, *nor does he if he intends,* commit any democrat to his moral convictions."

Speech of Hon. S. S. Cox, of Ohio, in the House of Representatives, Jan. 12, 1865.

"The democratic party of the free states are neither the advocates nor the apologists for slavery. Democracy and slavery are natural enemies. Impressed with the value of free labor, there is not a democrat in the North who would not resist the establishment of slavery in a free state."

Speech of Hon. William S. Holman, of Indiana, in the House of Representatives, Jan. 13, 1865.

"I have ever believed slavery wrong. The North have always believed it. Hardly one can at present be found who will claim that slavery is now, or has ever been, other than an evil. * * * The South, by rebellion, has absolved the democratic party at the North from all obligation to stand up longer for the defence of its 'corner-stone.' They are now using the very system which this amendment proposes to abolish, for the overthrow of our government, founded on the broad principles of right, justice, and humanity."

* * * * * * *

"I cannot but conclude, from the best light I can obtain, that the *operation of this measure will be most beneficial to the non-slaveholding white population of the Southern States.*. When these poorer laboring classes shall no longer have to contend with and struggle against and be degraded by slave labor, then, and not until then, will they come into the enjoyment of blessings such as are now fully enjoyed by the honest, toiling workingmen of the North.

"When labor shall be free at the South, then will it command and have the respect which is its just due. Then will millions of the white men of the North participate and share in the blessings thus secured. The masses of our native and foreign-born laborers, now toiling in the severer climate of the North, will be invited to enter upon these newly-opened fields, for their industry and occupation. The now hidden resources of the States South will be developed by the brain and muscle of the northern laborer.

"The existence in our country of antagonistic systems of labor has brought upon the nation the terrible calamity of a wasting civil war, with all its desolations. It has cost the country the lives of hundreds of thousands of its best and bravest sons, and has wasted her material resources.

"The day has come when this conflict of labor is to end, and the question is forced upon us by the South. They alone are resposible for it."

Speech of Hon. M. F. Odell, of New York, in the House of Representatives, Jan. 9th, 1865.

"I am opposed to the re-admission into the Union, with the rights of slave property of any State which our triumphant armies have subjected."

Speech of Hon. Elijah Ward, of New York, in the House of Representatives, Jan. 9th, 1865.

"I believe, and have ever believed since I was capable of thought, that it is a great affliction to any country where it prevails; and, so believing, I can never vote for any measure calculated to enlarge its area, or to render more permanent its duration. In some latitudes, and for some agricultural staples, slave labor may be, to the master, the most valuable species of labor, though this I greatly doubt. In others, and particularly in my own State, I am convinced that it is the very dearest species of labor; and in all, as far as national wealth and power and happiness are concerned, I am persuaded it admits of no comparison with the labor of freemen; and, above all, disguise it as we may, if the laws of population shall not be changed by Providence, or man's nature shall not be changed, it is an institution, sooner or later, pregnant with fearful peril.

    *   *   *   *   *   *   *

"I shall not stop to inquire, as I before intimated, whether the institution has produced the present war or not. However that may be, one thing, in my judgment, is perfectly clear, now that the war is upon us: *that a prosperous and permanent peace cannot be secured if the institution is permitted to survive.*

    *   *   *   *   *   *   *

"As we at present are, I cease to hope that the government can be restored and preserved so as to accomplish the great ends for which it was established, unless slavery be extinguished.

    *   *   *   *   *   *   *

"If suffered to continue, it will ever prove a fruitful topic of excitement and danger to our continuing peace and union. Terminate it, and the imagination of man, I think, is unable to conceive of any other subject which can give rise to fratricidal strife.

    *   *   *   *   *   *   *

"I think the honor and good name as well as the interest and safety of the country require, the abolition of slavery throughout our limits."

Speech of Hon. Reverdy Johnson, of Maryland, in the United States Senate, April 5th, 1864.

"The question of slavery is rapidly diminishing in importance; whether for good or evil, it is passing away."

Speech of Hon. D. W. Voorhees, of Indiana, in the House of Representatives, Jan. 9th, 1865.

Mr. Yeaman, of Kentucky, justified "anti-slavery measures" by quoting a letter signed by John J. Crittenden, William T. Barry, R. C. Anderson, J. Cabell Breckinridge, G. Robertson, John Rowen and B. W. Patton, all of Kentucky, urging the nomination of Henry Clay to the Presidency, and saying of Clay:

"We apprehend that no mistake could be greater than that

which would impute to him the wish to extend the acknowledged evils of slavery; for we are persuaded that no one entertains a stronger sense of its mischiefs than he does, or a more ardent desire, by all prudent and constitutional means, to extirpate it from our land."

Mr. Yeaman added: "Shall a man be told that it is wrong or disgraceful to hold opinions that have been sanctioned by the minds and hearts of such men."
Speech of Hon. George H. Yeaman, of Kentucky, in the House of Representatives, Jan. 9th, 1865.

"Slavery is the chief lever by which the rebel leaders have wielded the Southern mind; and for that reason it has lost nearly all the sympathy and support it once maintained."
Speech of Hon. Austin A. King, of Missouri, in the House of Representatives, Jan. 13th, 1865.

"At the last session I voted against the proposed amendment, but when the question is again taken, I intend to record my name in the affirmative."
* * * * * * *
"We never can have peace until we in some way dispose of the institution."
Speech of Hon. James S. Rollins, of Missouri, in the House of Representatives, Jan. 14th, 1865.

"The demoratic party never advocated slavery as a moral institution. That is a question which will not admit of discussion."
New York Leader, (organ of Tammany Hall,) Jan. 7th, 1865.

"The triumphs of our army and navy have put the rebels in such straits that they no longer refuse to listen to propositions of peace; and the plan of getting rid of slavery legally by a constitutional amendment which shall recognise and respect the rights of States, is a democratic measure, suggested by democrats, and it ought to be supported by democrats."
New York Leader, (organ of Tammany Hall,) Jan. 14th, 1865.

How Slavery Injures Free Workingmen.

The slave-labor system gives to the capitalist many unjust advantages over the poor free workman; it gives to a dozen slave-owners, with a thousand slaves, as many votes in the Legislature, and as great a political power in the State as is possessed by five hundred free workingmen; it discourages schools, prevents the formation of villages and towns; and gives to slave mechanics, slave shoemakers, slave blacksmiths, slave carpenters, slave wheelwrights, the labor, and to their wealthy masters the profits, which of right belong to the free workingman. To quote the words of the governor of a slave state, Governor Cannon, of Delaware, "Slave labor is uncompensated, white labor is compensated; when the two are brought into competition, white labor is crowded out. If capital owns its labor, the avenues to honest livelihood are forever closed to the white."

When a slave commits murder in Virginia, or any of the other Slave States, he is hanged, and his owner is paid for him the price he could have sold him for before the crime was committed. He is paid for the slave out of the treasury of the State; that is to say, *the tax-payers pay the slaveholder for his slave.*

When a farmer's bull does mischief and is killed, does the State pay the farmer? When a farmer's horse becomes unmanageable and is killed, does the State pay for him? Not at all. It is only the slave, the peculiar property of the rich, for whom the tax-payers are taxed. The poor man's horse or cow may be killed without payment to the owner.

FREE WORKINGMEN, AS SLAVE-GUARDS.

In the Slave States, whether in the city or in the country, a patrol of the white men is kept up at night—for what? To secure the persons and property of free workingmen? Not at all; but *to look after the slaves of the rich*: to prevent the slaves from running away; to keep them from visiting strange plantations; to catch them and bring them back, if they stray into the woods. "An ordinance organizing and establishing patrols for the police of slaves in the Parish Court of St. Landry, in Louisiana," which lies before us, describes minutely the organization of such patrols. "Every free white male person, between the ages of 16 and 60," is bound to do patrol duty. The parish (county) is to pay for "all books, blanks, papers, laws, &c., required for the organization of the patrols." Captains of patrols are to see that the enrollment for this duty includes every man; and anyone who neglects or refuses to serve, "at any hour of the day or night" which may be appointed, shall be fined or imprisoned. Six pages of the pamphlet are then taken up with defining the powers and duties of the patrols towards the slaves. They have no other duty to perform, as the title, indeed, asserts. They are "patrols for the police of the slaves." They are not to look out for horse-thieves, or to hunt for stolen cattle; it is made no part of their duty to guard the lives and property of the white workingmen of the county. "Every free white male, between 16 to 60," in the county is required to mount guard over the peculiar property of the few wealthy planters.

Now the parish of St. Landry had, in 1860, according to the census, 10,703 whites, and 11,436 slaves. According to the last census there were 3,953,587 slaves, and somewhat less than 400,000 slaveholders in the country—an average of ten slaves to each owner. At that rate the slaves in the parish of St. Landry would be owned by eleven hundred and forty-three of the 10,703 whites (for children and women own slaves as well as men); and *the whole free population of the county was taxed, in time, labor, and money, to care for the property of a little more than a tenth, and those the wealthiest part.*

Do not suppose that the white workingmen of the Slave States have not felt the oppression of this burden. Where they have been permitted, they have complained. Thus, in an address of Mr. Pierpoint, of Virginia, delivered in 1860, he remarked :

"The clerk or mechanic needs no protection of the law ; he is one of the sovereign *body guard to protect and keep in subordination the master's slaves.* Yet his income—the labor of his weary hand and aching head, is *taxed two per cent.* to buy arms and erect armories in which to manufacture the munitions of war, *with which to equip himself, to defend the master in his right to his slaves.*"

An address to the working people of Virginia, in 1860, called attention to the fact that " if a bull or a steer of one of our farmers becomes vicious, so as to be a public nuisance, he is ordered by the law to be killed, and his loss falls upon his owner, and upon him alone ; but if it happens that a slave of one of the Eastern Virginia capitalists becomes vicious and commits crime, he is hanged or transported, and *it is provided by law that his owner shall be paid his assessed value out of the State Treasury.*"

The appropriation, by the Virginia Legislature, in 1856, for patrols, and as pay to slave owners for vicious slaves hanged or transported, amounted to over forty thousand dollars ! At the same time, every laboring man in the State, with an income above $250 per annum, had to pay a heavy income tax, while the slaves of the rich were almost totally exempted from taxation.

THE FREE LABORER AND THE SLAVE.

The system of bond-labor is *antagonistic to that of free labor,* and breeds in the masters a contempt for the workingman, as well as for his vocation. This is perfectly natural, and indeed unavoidable. *The slave-owner is a competitor in the slave-market against the free workingman.* He lives upon the labor of his slaves, and he regards with dislike the free laborers who come into the market to bid against him and the labor he controls.

This fact is notorious in the South. It has long attracted the attention of free white workingmen there, but they have been too weak to resist the powerful slave-holders. In 1860, Robert C. Tharin, of Alabama, once a law-partner of the notorious William L. Yancey, endeavored to set up a newspaper called the *Non-Slaveholder,* to urge the passage of a law forbidding the employment of slaves except in agricultural labor and as servants. He thus sought to protect the free mechanics, and secure them employment. *For this Mr. Tharin was summarily driven from the State.*

Mr. Tharin, exposing the sopistries of William L. Yancey, writes:

"He had seen the rich man's negro 'come in contact' with the poor white blacksmith, the poor white bricklayer, carpenter, wheelright, and agriculturist. *He had seen the preference invariably given to the rich man's negro* in all such pursuits and trades; like me, *he* had heard the *complaints* of the poor white mechanic of the South against this very negro equality the rich planters were rapidly bringing about. These things he had heard and seen in Charleston, New Orleans, Mobile, Montgomery, and Wetumpka

"Have not the planters *for years condemned every mechanic in the South to negro equality?*" exclaims Mr. Tharin. "I never *envied* the planters of Wetumpka, or, indeed, of any part of the South. My *dislike* to them arose from their contemptible meanness, their utter disregard of decency, their supercilious arrogance, and their daily usurpations of powers and privileges at variance with my rights, and the rights of my class."

FREE WORKINGMEN MUST GIVE WAY TO SLAVES.

In 1853 the free mechanics of Concord, Cabarras county, North Carolina, held a meeting, at which they complained that the "*wealthy owners of slave mechanics were in the habit of under-bidding them in contracts.*" The free mechanic who led in this movement was driven from the town. A Long Island carpenter removed to a southern town; he was asked for an estimate for certain work in his trade. The person who proposed to have it done demurred at the price, and remarked that *he could do better to* buy *a carpenter, let him do the work* and sell him again when it was done. The free carpenter, being a man of sense, packed up his tools and returned to New York, where a rich man cannot *buy* a carpenter and sell him again.

Olmsted relates, in his "Texas Journey," that at Austin, the capital of the state, the German mechanics complained that when the labor for building the state capital was given out, many of them came with offers, but *were underbid by the owners of slave-mechanics.* But when the free mechanics had left town, in search of employment elsewhere, the slave owners threw up their contracts, and, having no longer any opposition, obtained new contracts at advanced prices.

In the iron mines and furnaces near the Cumberland river, in Tennessee, before the war, several thousand men found employment—but almost without an exception they were slaves. One company had a capital of $700,000—and owned seven hundred slaves. *Of course an equal number of free workmen were robbed of employment,* and had either to starve, or emigrate to the Free States, as so many thousands have done.

THE "FAT" FOR THE SLAVE, AND THE "LEAN" FOR THE FREE WORKINGMAN.

Printers call that work which is most quickly and easily done, and which is the best paid, " fat ; " that which is hard to do and poorly paid, they call " lean." Now, in all mechanical and other labor performed in the Slave States, the slave constantly gets the best, the easiest—the *fat;* the free mechanic or laborer, if he is employed at all, gets only the leavings of the slave, the *lean.* This comes about, because the slave-owner is a wealthy and influential man, who is able to select the lightest tasks for his slave; by this the slave-owner of course makes the greatest profit, and incurs the least expense. But the free white workingman must stand aside, or take that task which the slave-owner will not have.

In Virginia, a wealthy slave-owner told Olmsted that he used Hussey's reaper rather than McCormick's, because " it was more readily repaired by the *slave-blacksmith* on the farm." Another planter in Virginia employed a gang of Irishmen in draining some land. But mark the reasons he gave for this use of free labor. " It's dangerous work" (unwholesome), said he ; "and *a negro's life is too valuable to be risked at it.* If a negro dies, it is a considerable loss, you know." This slaveholder did not care how many Irishmen died in his malarious ditches. So, too, on the southwestern steamboats, *slaves* are employed to do the *lightest* and *least dangerous labor ;* but *Irish and German free workingmen are employed to perform the exhausting and dan-*

gerous work. Thus, on the Alabama river, Olmsted observed that slaves were sent upon the bank to roll down cotton bales, but Irishmen were kept below to drag them away. The mate of the boat said, by way of explanation, " The niggers are worth too much to be risked here; *if the Paddies are knocked overboard, or get their backs broke, nobody loses anything.*"

Alfred E. Matthews, of Starke county, Ohio, in his " Journal of his Flight" from Mississippi, in 1861, remarks: "*I have seen free white mechanics obliged to stand aside while their families were suffering for the necessaries of life, when slave mechanics, owned by rich and influential men, could get plenty of work;* and I have heard these same white mechanics breathe the most bitter curses against the institution of slavery and the slave aristocracy." In his journal at Columbus, Mississippi, he writes : " Business is very dull. Many of the free white mechanics have nothing to do, and there is a great deal of suffering amongst them. *Most of what little work is to be done is given to the slave mechanics.* An intelligent carpenter, an acquaintance of one of the persons in the office where I was engaged, came up one day and told his friend that his family were suffering for provisions; he had no money, and could not get work at anything. He assured me this was the case with others of his acquaintance." This was in a town of three thousand five hundred inhabitants.

SLAVES ARE TRAINED TO MECHANICAL PURSUITS.

On a rice plantation in South Carolina the planter showed Mr. Olmsted "shops and sheds at which blacksmiths, carpenters, and other mechanics—all slaves—were at work." Of course, *this planter employed no free mechanics.* Indeed, the writer of this pamphlet was told by a wealthy Alabamian in 1860, that *the planters* in his region were *determined to discontinue altogether the employment of free mechanics.* " On my own place," said this person, " I have now slave carpenters, slave blacksmiths, and slave wheelrights, and thus *I am independent of free mechanics.*"

These instances, culled from southern life, show the bearing of the slave system upon the free working population. The planters do not need the assistance of the free laboring class; they despise it, and discourage it. What is the result ? Let "mudsill" Hammond, Governor of South Carolina, bear witness. In an address before the South Carolina Institute, some years ago, he said :

" According to the best calculations which, in the absence of statistic facts, can be made, it is believed that of the three hundred thousand white inhabitants of South Carolina there are not less than fifty thousand whose industry, such as it is, is not in the present condition of things, and does not promise hereafter, such a support as every white person in this country is and feels himself entitled to."

In another part of his address he said : "Eighteen or at most nineteen dollars will cover the whole necessary annual cost of a full supply of wholesome and palatable food, purchased in the market," for one person in South Carolina. It would seem, therefore, that so *completely had the slave system robbed the free workingman of the opportunity to make an honest livelihood, that one-sixth of the free white population of South Carolina could not earn even the paltry sum of eighteen dollars per annum !* So completely have the slaveholders monopolized the labor market for their slaves !

The bitter hatred of the " free white" in the South for the negro has been often spoken of. Does any one wonder at it, when he considers that these free men feel the wrongs they suffer, but are too ignorant to trace them to their sources ? They hate the slaves, but if they were somewhat more intelligent they would hate the slaveholders, who are the authors of all their woes. It is because Mr. Lincoln, himself a southern man, and a son of one of the oppressed and expatriated free workingmen of the South, understands this, that he will not suffer the re-establishment of the iniquitous class of monopolists of labor, whose hatred for free workingmen has dragged the country into a civil war. He aims, not so much to free the slave, as *to free the workingmen.* He sees, as a statesman, that a system which degrades and discourages free labor, and whose supporters hate and refuse to employ free workingmen, is ruinous to the prosperity of the country, and is necessarily the parent of constant dissensions, the fruitful source of hatreds, jealousies and heart-burnings. He knows as a statesman, that the security of free government rests upon the virtue, intelligence and prosperity of the working class :

2

and that if we desire the perpetuity of our Union and liberties, we must sweep out of the way a system whose constant and necessary tendency is to impoverish and debase the free workingman.

WHY FREE WORKINGMEN HATE THE SLAVES.

They hate the slaves because slavery oppresses them. Turn where he will, the southern *free mechanic and laborer finds the negro slave preferred before him.* The planter has his slave blacksmith, his slave carpenter, his slave wheelwright, his slave engineer, if he needs one. It is now as it was in Marion's day, who said : " The people of Carolina form two classes—the rich and the poor. The poor are generally very poor, because, *not being necessary to the rich, who have slaves to do all their work*, they get no employment from them."

The slaveholders have the political power ; they look only to their own interests ; and even where they have established manufactures, they have given work by preference to slaves over free men and women. " *We are beginning to manufacture with slaves*," wrote Governor Hammond of South Carolina, in 1845, to Thomas Clarkson. A writer in the Augusta *Constitutionalist*, quoted approvingly by De Bow, in 1852, said, " for manufacturing in the hot and lower latitudes, slaves are peculiarly qualified, and *the time is approaching when they will be sought as the operative most to be preferred and depended on.* I could name factories in South Carolina, Alabama and Georgia, where the success of *black* labor has been encouraging." At the Saluda Factory, near Columbia, South Carolina, so long ago as 1851, one hundred and twenty-eight operatives were employed—*all slaves.* " Slaves not sufficiently strong to work in the cotton fields can attend to the looms and spindles," wrote the superintendent of this mill ; and he showed how these slaves underworked the free whites :

" Average cost of a slave operative, per annum......... $75
" Average cost of a white operative, at least........... 106
                                                        ————
    " Difference $31

" Or over thirty per cent. saved in the labor alone by using only the weakly and deformed slaves."

Free labor is killed by such unnatural competition. A writer upon manufactures in the South, in 1852, compared the wages paid to operatives in Tennessee with those in Lowell; "In Lowell, labor is paid the fair compensation of eighty cents per day for men, and two dollars per week for women, while in Tennessee the average compensation for labor does not exceed fifty cents per day for men, and one dollar and twenty-five cents per week for women." Another writer said : "A female operative in the New England cotton factories receives from ten to twelve dollars per month; *this is more than a female slave generally hires for in the southwest.*" This was twelve years ago. But he goes on to explain how *the slaveholder,* monopolizing the labor of his slaves, has the power to control the labor market and *underbid the free workman under any circumstances.* "It matters nothing to him (the slaveholder) how low others can produce the article ; he can produce it lower still, so long as it is the best use he can make of his labor, and so long as that labor is worth keeping." That is to say, a free white mechanic is at the mercy of his neighbor, the capitalist, in a slave state, because, *if the capitalist does not like his price, he can* " *go and buy a carpenter and sell him again when the work is done.*" Thus, while it is true that in the long run and on the average free labor is always cheaper than slave labor, the capitalist who monopolizes the slave labor is able to *drive out or starve out the free laborer,* over whom he and his slaves have an unfair advantage. The slaveholders used to boast that there were no "strikes" in the South—here we see the reason. The writer we have quoted adds :

"*It is a fact that slaves learn blacksmithing, carpentering, boot and shoemaking, and in fact all handicraft trades, with as much facility as white men ; and Mr. Deering of Georgia, has employed slaves in his cotton factory for many years with de- cided success.*"

FREE WORKINGMEN ARE "PESTS TO SOCIETY.

Olmstead, when he asked in the slave states why the white laboring men were not employed, was told that they were not hired "because you cannot *drive* them as you do a slave." *The aristocratic slave-owner refuses to employ a workman whom he cannot flog and curse.* On a rice plantation in South Carolina he found a *slave engineer*, for whose education in that profession his owner had paid five hundred dollars to a steam-engine builder. This slave machinist, an able man, *lived better than any laboring free white man in the district.* His master, who also owned slave blacksmiths, carpenters, and other mechanics, *did not employ a single freeman*, except an overseer. But an estate of the same size and value in a free state would have given employment to twenty-five or thirty white mechanics of different trades, not to speak of a large number of free laborers.

By the census of 1850 it appears that the average wages of the female operatives in the Georgia cotton factories were $7 39 per per month; in Massachusetts it was $14 57 per month. New England factory girls were induced by the special offer of high wa es to go to Georgia to work in newly-established cotton factories, but they found the position so unpleasant, owing to the general degradation of the laboring class, they were very soon forced to return. Nor shall we wonder at this when we read the following sentiment, which appeared in the Charleston *Standard*, in 1855:

"*A large portion of the mechanical force that migrate to the South are a curse instead of a blessing;* they are generally a *worthless, unprincipled class*, enemies to our peculiar institution (slavery), and formidable barriers to the success of our native mechanics (slaves). Not so, however, with another class who migrate southward—we mean that class known as merchants; *they* are generally intelligent and trustworthy, and they seldom fail to discover their true interests. They become slaveholders and landed proprietors; and in ninety-nine cases out of a hundred they are better qualified to become constituents of our institution than a certain class of our native born, who from want of capacity are perfect drones in society, *continually carping about slave competition.* * * * The *mechanics*, the most of them, are *pests to society*, dangerous among the slave population, and ever ready to form combinations against the interests of the slaveholder."

Is it strange that the ignorant, neglected, despised free white workingman of the slave states hates the slave? He feels that the slave injures him in every possible way; the slave robs him of work; the slave deprives him of bread and clothing for his children; the slave gets the easiest tasks, the free laborer the hardest and most dangerous; the slave steps before him whenever he looks for a job, and has the preference everywhere, *because he is the tool of a capitalist whose influence and wealth enable him to grasp*—for his own benefit—whatever might be of advantage to the free mechanic or laborer.

The capitalist, in a slave state, is a man with a hundred black arms, all bare, all eagerly seeking work, all ready to work for less than a free man can support his family decently upon. The capitalist is a hundred-armed workman, with enough social influence to command work for all his hundred arms, *to the exclusion of the honest free mechanic and laborer.* The slave, in the hands of this capitalist, is the most dangerous enemy the free workman can have. Suppose a job of work for twenty mechanics is to be given out in a southern town—twenty free men offer themselves—but a slave-owner comes, with the prestige of great wealth, with his social influence and his political power, and he gets the preference for his twenty slaves, *the profits of whose labor go to make him richer, while his free neighbors grow poorer.* It is not strange that the southern free working-men resent this monstrous wrong—but it is lamentable that they make the error of hating the tools with which the wrong is done, and not those who use these helpless tools, and the iniquitous system which permits it. It is as though a martyr should abhor only the thumb-screws which torture him, but regard kindly the executioner who applies them; it is as though a western traveller should complain of the scalping knife, but love the Indian savage who uses it.

It is the slave-holder who wrongs the free workingman. It is the slave system which oppresses him. Make the slave free and he is no longer your fatal competitor; take the slaves away from the capitalist, and he has no longer the power to rob you of work and bread. Free the negroes, and you redeem the free white working-class from the domination of the selfish capitalists, and make the blacks themselves harmless to you. It is only while they are slaves that the negroes injure the white working men.

HOW FREE WORKINGMEN ARE OVERTAXED IN SLAVE STATES.

We have shown how the slave-labor system robs the free workingman, the free mechanic and laborer, of employment and bread, and thus keeps him poor and helpless—or drives him into the free states. But the subjection of free labor in slave states does not stop there. Not only is the free workingman condemned by the monopolists of slave labor to idleness and poverty, but his children are held in ignorance; his political rights are cunningly abridged; the products of his labor are forced to bear an *unequal* burden of taxation; and he—the non-slaveholding workingman—is compelled by the laws to mount guard over the slaves of his wealthy neighbor, or else to pay for such a guard. Thus he is injured in every interest, for the benefit of the slaveholder.

In the free states of the Union a poor man's vote counts as much as his wealthy neighbor's, and the millionaire enjoys no special political privileges over the carpenter who builds his house, or the blacksmith who shoes his horse. We are accustomed to think this a good system, but how is it in the slave states? Take Virginia as an example. There, while in one branch of the Legislature men are represented, in the other *money* and slaves have also a large representation.

So great was this political power of wealth, that before the war *ten thousand white men—slaveholders—in Eastern Virginia* had as much power—as many votes—in the Senate, as forty thousand white men—non-slaveholders—of Western Virginia.

How did the slaveholders, the aristocrats of Eastern Virginia, use this power? *They exempted a great part of their peculiar property from taxation,* and laid the burden of taxes upon the free workingmen of the state. They enacted a law by which all slaves under twelve years of age were exempted from taxation altogether—*but they taxed the calves, the colts, the lambs, of the farmers.* They limited the tax upon slaves over twelve years to one dollar and twenty cents per head; but they taxed a trader with a capital of only six hundred dollars, sixty dollars for his first year's license, and a heavy duty on his sales afterwards. The slave property of Virginia, before the war, paid about

$300,000 per annum taxes—but *if it had been taxed as other property was, according to value, it would have contributed one million three hundred thousand dollars per annum!* The odd million was raised by extra taxes on the earnings of the free laborers.

Not only this—the *products* of slave labor were also exempted from taxation. Tobacco, corn, wheat and oats were not taxed; but the product of free labor, consisting of cattle, hogs, sheep, &c., was heavily taxed; as were *also the earnings of free laboring men,* who were obliged to pay an income tax. It was asserted by Mr. Peirpoint, in 1860, that "upwards of two hundred and thirty million dollars of the Virginia slaveholders' capital in slaves was *exempted from taxation.*"

But while the slave owner was so protected, see how it fared with the free laborer? Every free mechanic, artisan, or laborer of whatever kind, who was in the employment of any person, was obliged, by a special law, to pay an income tax of *one-half of one per cent. if his income did not exceed* $250 : of one per cent. if his income was under $500; of one and a half per cent. if it was under $1,000, and two per cent. if he earned over $1,000. Our workingmen think the United States income tax onerous; but that, at least, exempts the man who earns less than $600. *The Virginia slaveholders exempted only themselves!* They taxed the poor, but left the the rich to pay nothing.

ENORMOUS AND UNEQUAL TAXATION OF FREE WORKINGMEN IN VIRGINIA.

See how this act worked. In Wheeling there were employed in 1859 about 1,500 free men in the iron mills; these earned an average of $400 per annum each. On this they had to pay one per cent.—four dollars—making $6,000 per annum; besides eighty cents poll tax, $1,200 more; total $7,200, drawn from 1,500 free laboring men. Now *this tax was equal to that levied on six thousand slaves.* That is to say, each free workman was taxed four times as heavily as a slave. But take note of this: the owner of the slave was not only very lightly taxed for his property in him; *he paid no income tax at all.* That is to say, the net income from the labor of six thousand slaves might be reckoned in those times at $900,000 per annum. On this the masters, the capitalists, who received this sum, paid not a cent of income-tax! Or, take another example: a foreman in a factory earned $1,100 per annum; he had to pay $22 80 income tax to the State. But a slave-owning capitalist paid no more than that as his tax on nineteen slaves; *he trained them to mechanical work*—hired them out in such manner that they threw nineteen free mechanics out of employment—and on the proceeds of the labor of these nineteen slaves, amounting to $5,700 per annum, *he was taxed not a single cent!*

"There are many poor men in this State," said Mr. Pierpoint in 1860, "getting 75, 80, 90, and 100 cents per day, with families to support, who all have to pay, in addition to the income tax, for everything they own on the face of the earth, forty cents on a hundred dollars, while the slaveholder only pays 10 cents on the hundred dollars' worth of slaves!" "The income tax levied by the slaveholders upon the small incomes of free mechanics," Mr. Pierpoint said, "will eat out the very vitals of all the manufacturing energy of the State." Nor were the free mechanics the only sufferers. "The farmer in Western Virginia (not a slaveholder) who 12 years ago paid his tax with 15 dollars, now pays $60, with little increase in actual value." *Only the slaveholders were exempted!*

Thus was slave labor encouraged and free labor made penal in the South. Thus, to use Marion's words, the poor became poorer and the rich richer. Thus free mechanics were driven out of the slave states, taxed out, starved out, until, in 1859, Charleston, one of the chief seaports of the South, had not left so much as a single ship-carpenter. Thus was brought about the unhappy condition of the free workingmen, described by Mr. Tarver, in "DeBow's Industrial Resources of the South and Southwest."

"The acquisition of a respectable position in the scale of wealth appears so difficult that they decline the hopeless pursuit, and many of them settle down into passive idleness, and become the almost passive subjects of all its consequences. An evident deterioration is taking place in this part of the population; the younger portion of it being less educated, less industrious, and in every point of view less respectable than their ancestors."

HOW SLAVES OUT-VOTE FREE WORKINGMEN.

These are the effects of the slave labor system upon the unfortunate free laborers who are subject to its influence. Bear in mind that it is not only in Virginia that the free mechanic and laborer is thus wronged. In Louisiana, in South Carolina, in most of the slave states, slave property is represented and favored in some special manner. In Louisiana the representation, under the old system, was apportioned according to the whole population—free and slave. Thereby it happened that the thousands of free laborers of New Orleans were placed at the mercy of a few enormously wealthy slave-owning capitalists in the sparsely settled river parishes; and *a thousand votes of free mechanics had not so much power in the Legislature as two hundred and fifty planters' votes, whose slaves filled up a legislative district.*

South Carolina has always been called the model slave state. Her system was and is the admiration of the slaveholding class. There the free laborer was entirely debarred from influence, totally unrepresented. He could vote—but not for one of his own class; *only a slave owner could serve in the Legislature; only a slave owner could be governor; and the Legislature, composed exclusively of slave owners,* appointed the judges, the magistrates, the senators, the electors for President.

Not only this—the Legislature set apart the state Congressional districts; and it managed this in such manner that the slaveholding interest was alone represented in Congress. The lower part of the State, where the slaves were most dense, sent four out of the seven representatives to Congress. In the legislative apportionment the free workingmen of the State were still more outraged. Five-sixths of the white population, residing in those counties where there were but few slaves, had only seventy-eight out of one hundred and twenty-two representatives in the Legislature—a little more than one-half. The Pendleton district, with over twenty-six thousand white inhabitants, but few slaves, sent but seven members; the parishes of St. Philip and St. Michael, with less than nineteen thousand whites, but a heavy slave population, sent eighteen.

Now take notice of the results of this system upon the free

3

workingmen. Governor Seabrook, of South Carolina, said, in a message a few years ago :

"Education has been provided by the Legislature *but for one class of the citizens* of the State, which is *the wealthy class.* For the middle and poorer classes of society it has done nothing, since no organized system has been adopted for that purpose. * * * * * Ten years ago twenty thousand adults, besides ch: .en, were unable to read or write, in South Carolina. Has our free school system dispelled any of this ignorance? Are there not reasonable fears to be entertained that the number has increased since that period ?"

In the Charleston *Standard*, in November, 1855, was advanced by eminent South Carolinians the atrocious doctrine that the State should educate only its capitalists and the officers and overseers who, under the order of the capitalists, should command and direct the laborers. Chancellor Harper, one of the foremost men of the State, said, in a public address printed by De Bow, and received with general approval :

"Would you do a benefit to the horse, or the ox, by giving him a cultivated understanding or fine feelings? So far as the *mere laborer* has the pride, the knowledge, and the aspiration of a free man, he is unfitted for his situation, and must doubly feel its infelicity."

And what was the effect of this system upon the free workingmen of the State? Let Governor Hammond, one of its chief citizens, reply. Fifty thousand, he said, a sixth of the white population of the State, *were unable to earn their living.* He added : "Most of them now follow agricultural pursuits, *in feeble but injurious competition with slave labor.*" And another writer, whose essay on cotton and cotton manufactures at the South is printed by De Bow, remarks that " a degree and extent of poverty and destitution exist in the Southern States among a certain class of people, almost unknown in the manufacturing districts of the North. * * * Boys and girls by thousands, destitute both of employment and the means of education, grow up to ignorance and poverty, and too many of them to vice and crime."

Such are some—but not all—the disabilities under which the

free workingman labors, in a State where the slave-labor system prevails. Deprived of employment, left without education, misrepresented in the legislative halls by men whose interests are opposed to his, and before whom he is powerless, the free laborer grows poorer as his wealthy neighbor grows richer; and looking at these things we cease to wonder at the persistent emigration from the eastern slave states, westward, of which Mr. Tarver said, speaking of South Carolina, " That necessity must be strong and urgent which induces *thirty per cent. of the population of a State, in the short space of ten years, to break all the social and individual ties which bind man to the place of his birth, and seek their fortunes in other lands.*"

FREE WORKINGMEN FLY FROM THE SLAVE STATES.

The slave states are the most sparsely populated of the Union ; their soil is rich, their climate kindly, they abound in mineral wealth ; everything there favors the workingman—yet the workingmen of the free states refuse to go there ; and a *constant and large stream of emigration has set for years, from the slave states into the free states.* The free workingmen of the slave states have fled from the oppression and blight of the slave institution, to the part of the Union where all labor is free and paid.

If we take the census report of 1850, we find that the slave states had sent nearly six times as many of their population into free territory as the free states had sent into slave territory. We find that Kentucky had sent on to free soil sixty thousand more persons than all the free states had sent into slave soil. Little Maryland had sent more than half as many persons into free territory as all the slave states had sent into slave territory. Virginia had sent sixty thousand more persons into free territory than all the free states had sent upon the slave soil. Kentucky and Tennessee were but little behind the other states we have mentioned.

This shows the course of emigration. But it is even more clearly shown in some interesting tables contained in the last census report—that for 1860. In a table of " Internal Migration" we find that there were in the country, and returned by the census-takers, 399,700 persons born in Virginia, but *living in other states;* 344,765 persons born in Tennessee, but living in other states; 272,606 persons born in North Carolina, but living in other states; 137,258 persons born in Maryland, but living in other states; 32,493 persons born in Delaware, but living in other states; 331,904 persons born in Kentucky, but living in other states.

Now it is true that not all these 1,518,726 persons who had migrated from only the border line of slave states were living in the free states, but by far the greater number were. The "course of internal migration" is exhibited in a table of the Census Report. There we find that emigrants from Virginia have removed "chiefly" to Ohio, Missouri, Kentucky, and Indiana; from Kentucky they have removed chiefly to Missouri, Indiana, Illinois and Ohio. From Maryland they have removed chiefly to Ohio, Pennsylvania, Virginia and the District of Columbia. From Delaware they have migrated chiefly to Pennsylvania, Maryland, Ohio and Indiana. From Tennessee they have removed chiefly to Missouri, Arkansas, Texas and Illinois.

But this table shows us a far more remarkable fact. From the southern tier of slave states the migration was chiefly into other slave states, in a western or northwestern direction *towards the free states.* From the border slave states the migration was *chiefly into the free states,* and into that slave state (Missouri) which promised first to become free. But from the free states, which sent forth also a large stream of emigrants, there was *no* emigration to slave states; *all,* with insignificant exceptions, removed to *other free states.* 399,700 Virginians had removed chiefly to Ohio, Missouri, Kentucky and Indiana; but of 582,512 Pennsylvanians, just across the line, it is recorded that they removed "chiefly" to Ohio, Illinois, Indiana, and Iowa. 331,904 Kentuckians had removed "chiefly" to Missouri, Indiana, Illinois and Ohio; but 593,043 persons born across the river, in free Ohio, had removed chiefly to Indiana, Illinois, Iowa and Missouri. These contrasts hold good of the whole table. From no free state has there been emigration to the slave states; but from every border slave state there has been a very heavy migration to the free states.

Observe, that this course of migration is unusual and unnatural.

The tendency, in all the history of the world, has been the other way. Tribes and families have fled from the bleak climate and barren soil of the North to the milder climate and more generous soil of the South. A French writer, the Count de Segur, says: "The human race does not march in that direction; it turns its back to the North; the sun attracts its regards, its desires, and its steps. It is no easy matter to arrest this great current." In other countries all emigration has turned to the Southward, by an instinctive movement; but with us the horror of slavery, the aversion of the free laborer to come in contact and competition with slave labor, has sufficed to conquer even this strong instinctive tendency.

Bear in mind, too, that the South has lost, by this migration, the best class of her citizens. The indolent masters remained; the slaves remained; those free whites who were too poor and helpless and ignorant either to desire or to be able to remove, remained; but there has been a constant drain of the yeomanry of the border slave states—the forehanded farmers and industrious mechanics, the class whom a state can least afford to lose. These men and their families have helped to fill our northwestern territories and states; and have taken the places of the thousands who removed from the border free states to the northwest. They have faced unwonted winters and harder conditions of life—why? Because *these free workingmen felt slavery to be a curse, a bar to all their efforts.* They were not abolitionists—they brought into the free states with them their curious hatred of the negro, as though it was the slave and not the master who was their oppressor.

SLAVERY EXTERMINATES FREE MECHANICS.

Charles J. Faulkner, of Virginia, said, in 1832, in the legislature of that state: "*Slavery banishes free white labor; it exterminates the mechanic, the artisan, the manufacturer, it deprives them of bread.*" And C. C. Clay, of Alabama, not less eminent in the South than Mr. Faulkner, said a few years ago: "Our wealthier planters, with greater means and no more skill, are buying out their poorer neighbors, extending their plantations and adding to their force. The wealthy few, who are able to live on smaller profits, and to give their blasted fields some rest, are thus pushing off the many who are merely independent. Thus *the white population has decreased, and the slave increased,* almost *pari passu* in several counties of our state. In 1825 Madison county cast about three thousand votes; now she cannot cast more than two thousand three hundred. In travelling that country one will discover numerous *farm-houses, once the abode of industrious and intelligent freemen, now occupied by slaves,* or tenantless, deserted, and dilapidated. He will see the moss growing on the mouldering walls of once thrifty villages, and will find 'one only master grasps the whole domain,' that once furnished happy homes for a dozen white families."

Thus southern men, themselves slaveholders, bear witness to the causes which lead to the great and constant migration of the most valuable class of citizens from the slave to the free states. The agriculturist and the mechanic alike, the blacksmith, the carpenter, the farmer, all are "pushed off," to use the expressive phrase of Mr. Clay, to make way for the masters and their slaves.

SLAVERY SHUTS THE SOUTH AGAINST GERMANS AND IRISHMEN.

If a considerable part of the white workingmen of the slave states have migrated to the free states, it is equally true that of the thousands of German, Irish and other workingmen who have, with their families, sought our shores, the southern states have received but an insignificant fraction.

To the industry and thrift of this part of our population a large share of our prosperity and wealth is owing; without the help of their strong arms, the free states, though thriving and populous, and receiving increase from the South, must have advanced much more slowly than they have. This fact has been generally recognized amongst us. Indeed, in the western states special inducements have been held out to immigrants, so strongly have the people there felt the need of their labor and the advantage of their presence. Consider, then, what has been the loss of the South, which has utterly failed to attract this class, while at the same time it was drained to a considerable extent of its own free working class.

If we compare free states with slave states, we find that while

South Carolina had in 1860 but 9,986 foreign born citizens. Massachusetts had 260,114; Virginia had but 35,058 foreigners, but Pennsylania, her neighbor, had 430,505; Georgia, the empire state of the South, had but 11,671, but New York had 998,640; Mississippi had only 8,558, but Illinois had 324,643, Tennessee had 21,226, and Kentucky 59,799; but Ohio had 328,254, and Indiana 118,184. Little Rhode Island, with an insignificant territory and a dense population of 133 to the square mile, had attracted 37,394 foreign emigrants; but North Carolina, with a milder and more varied climate, a fertile soil, ready access by sea, and the advantage of a profitable fishery and several other special pursuits, not to speak of an immensely greater territory, had been able to attract to her borders but 3,299 foreign emigrants.

Nor must we fail to notice that in those states where slavery languished or had but a slender hold, emigrants at once increased in numbers. Maryland had 77,536, nearly seven times as many as Georgia; Delaware had 9,165, nearly three times as many as North Carolina; and Missouri had 160,541, as many within fifteen thousand as all the slave states east of the Mississippi, except Maryland and Delaware. That is to say, Missouri, which was in the popular belief certain to become a free state before many years, was able to attract to her soil nearly as many emigrants as Kentucky, Tennessee, Mississippi, Alabama, Georgia, North and South Carolina and Virginia together! Still, slavery told against Missouri when compared with the free states. With a milder climate, immensely greater mineral resources, and a nearer and cheaper access to great markets, Missouri had attracted but 13.59 per cent. of foreigners, while Iowa had 15.71 per cent., Minnesota 33.78 per cent., and Wisconsin 35.69 per cent.

The census report shows that of the foreign born population the free states have received over eighty-six and one-half per cent., and the slave states less than fourteen. It shows the States which have received the smallest percentage of this accretion to be North Carolina, Arkansas, Mississippi, Georgia, and South Carolina—*all slave states.* And it shows also the singular fact, that while eight foreign emigrants have settled in the free states to one in the slave states, the number of slaves—if we add the insignificant number of free colored—gives just one to every eight of our population.

FREE WORKINGMEN KEPT OUT OF THE FINEST PART OF THE UNION.

Is it no matter to workingmen that they are thus driven out and kept out of the largest, most fertile, and pleasantest part of the Union by the slave-labor system, which there robs them of work, and attacks their rights? In the mild climate of the border slave states, the seasons are longer, the productions more varied; trades which can be pursued in the North during only eight or nine months, may be carried on there all the year round; food is or ought to be cheaper; the workingman and his family need fewer and less costly clothes; in many ways the conditions of life are easier, for the mechanic and laborer as well as the farmer, than in the colder North. *But that great region the slavemasters closed against the free working men,* and preserved for themselves and their slaves.

The climate is not too hot in any of those states for white men and women to labor in the fields. Governor Hammond, of South Carolina, said: "The steady heat of our summers is not so prostrating as the short but sudden and frequent heats of northern summers." White men work on the levee in New Orleans in midsummer, and have the severest labor put upon them at that. He who writes this has rolled cotton and sugar upon the levee of New Orleans in the month of July, and screwed cotton in Mobile Bay in August. Dr. Cartwright, the great apostle of slavery, rightly remarked: "*Here in New Orleans the large part of the drudgery—work requiring exposure to the sun, as railroad making, street paving, dray driving, ditching, and building is performed by white people.*" This severe labor was put upon the free white workingmen; the slave-owners reserved the light tasks for their slaves.

In Alabama, by the census of 1850, sixty-seven thousand, in Mississippi, fifty-five thousand, in Texas forty-seven thousand *white men, non-slaveholders, labored in the fields,* and took no hurt. Cotton was cultivated in Texas, before the war, with perfect success, by white men; the Germans managed even to raise more pounds to the acre, pick it cleaner, and to get a higher price for it, than the neighboring planters. Olmsted mentions an American in Texas who would not employ slave labor, and who, with white men as his help, "produced more bales to the hand than any planter around him."

The mortality reports of the census show that the southern states are not peculiarly unhealthful. In Alabama, the deaths, per cent., were less than in Connecticut; in Georgia they are 1.23 per cent., in New York, 1.22 ; in South Carolina they are 1.44 per cent., in Massachusetts, 1.76, which is precisely the same as in Louisiana, notoriously, till General Butler cleaned New Orleans and drove out the yellow fever, the most sickly state in the South.

Nothing, therefore, has kept free workingmen out of these states—nearer to the great markets of the world, having more abundant mineral wealth, and in every way more favorably situated than the cold Northeast and the far away Northwest— except the fatal competition of the slaveowners. To avoid that, millions of workingmen, native and foreign born, have removed to the northwest, until at last the tide of emigration has even trenched upon the inhospitable desert, and has spread beyond the extreme limits of arable land, and far beyond the profitable reach of markets. The Northwestern farmer has burned his corn because he could not afford to send it to the distant sea-board—*was it no loss to him that slavery kept him out of the fertile fields of Virginia and North Carolina?*

Even had slavery remained in full vigor, the time had come when free labor, seeking new outlets and greater opportunities, would have pressed hardly upon it. If slavery is swept away, free workingmen will hereafter have opportunity in the South, and to all that great region a boundless future of wealth and prosperity opens up. The abandoned farms, the mouldering villages, the empty cottages, will once more be filled with the busy and cheerful hum of the labor of freemen.

Their cunning will repair the waste of unskillful slave labor; their ingenious toil will redeem the barren fields of Virginia and other southern states. The tide of emigration, sweeping in that direction, may repeat in the South the marvellous results which it has accomplished during the last twenty-five years in the Northwest; Virginia will be another Minnesota, North Carolina a new Iowa, and in Tennessee will be repeated the story of Ohio.

4

HOW TO LESSEN THE BURDEN OF TAXATION.

When a man falls into debt, and is anxious to free himself of it, what does he do? He works harder, and lives more frugally, He tries to make a dollar more per week, and to live on a dollar less. In that way he may hope to get clear of debt. Well, as with a man, so it is with a nation: we have incurred a great debt; and henceforth, we must, as a people, live more economically, and use, to better advantage, our property and our strength. We can no longer afford to exhaust our soil, by "artless" methods of culture; we can no longer afford to employ half a dozen men to do one man's work; we can no longer afford to use poor tools, to do with a hoe the work of a plough, to reap by hand instead of by steam, to work by main strength and stupidness, instead of intelligently.

It is not enough that one part of the country shall do its best—the resources of all parts must be fully developed. It is not fair to the working men of the free states, that they shall pay heavier taxes, in order that slaveholders may indulge their fancy for dull, plodding, unskilled slave labor. It is not fair that we of the North should bear a heavy burden, more than our proper share of the common debt, when, by the use of proper means, by throwing the Southern states open to free labor, and to skilled labor, its resources can be rapidly developed to the point where those states will be as populous, and as wealthy, as the free states.

If we can discover a way to make the whole country populous, and to make the whole nation prosperous, the weight of taxation will be much lightened; increased numbers and increased wealth will enable us to bear, without suffering, burdens under which we might sink if these elements of strength were lacking.

WE CANNOT AFFORD SLAVERY.

We cannot afford to omit measures which will add to our ability to pay taxes. There was a time when we might live after a slipshod fashion, but hereafter it is important to every man in the country, and especially to the workingmen and their families, that the natural resources of the whole country shall be

wisely and effectively developed. It is easy to show that the
Southern states have enormous and inexhaustible wealth of iron,
coal, copper, and many other things; but if that mineral wealth
is to remain, in future as in the past, in the bowels of the earth;
if Virginia, with the richest coal and iron deposits, is hereafter,
as heretofore, to buy both coal and iron in Pennsylvania; if
Tennessee, abounding in minerals, is to continue to be cursed
with a slave-labor system, which forbids the development of
her greatest sources of wealth; if we do not use the only means
in our power, or any one's power, to bring out that wealth, and
thus add enormously to the general wealth of the country—
which can only be done by extirpating slave-labor, and substitut-
ing free labor in its place—why then, we may as well reconcile
ourselves—we free working men of the North—to paying per-
petually much the heaviest share of the national taxation.

A shrewd foreign traveller once remarked that the slave-
labor system was such a costly economical blunder, that no
European nation could afford it; only a country having no debt,
and scarcely any expenses, could indulge in it. The time has
come when we, too, can no longer afford it. *If the working
men of the free states wish to lift from their backs some portion
of the heavy burden of taxation, they must insist that the southern states shall be thrown open to free labor,* in order that this
vast region shall be enabled to yield an equal share of the na
tional revenue. It cannot do this till it is equally wealthy; but,
as we shall proceed to show, the slave labor system has made it
poorer instead of richer, for many years.

How are we to equalize the burden? By making Virginia
as populous and wealthy as Pennsylvania, Kentucky as Ohio,
Tennessee and Georgia as New York, South Carolina as Massachusetts, Mississippi as Iowa. The Lynchburg *Virginian* wrote
some years ago:

"The coal fields of Virginia are the most extensive in the
world; and the coal is of the best and purest quality; her iron
deposits are altogether inexhaustible, and in many instances so
pure that it is malleable in its primitive state; and many of
these deposits are in the vicinity of extensive coal fields. She
has, too, very extensive deposits of copper, lead, and gypsum.
Her rivers are numerous and bold, generally with fall enough
for extensive water power."

VIRGINIA AND PENNSYLVANIA COMPARED.

But these coal and iron and copper and lead deposits of Virginia, greater than those of Pennsylvania, and lying in a finer climate, are almost untouched. And because they are so, the whole industry of the state has suffered. The census of 1850 gave the following values to agricultural lands in the adjoining States of Pennsylvania and Virginia :

	In Virginia.	In Penn'a.
Number of acres of improved land in farms	10,380,135	8,626,619
Number unimproved	15,792,176	6,294,728

Cash value of farms in Virginia, *eight* dollars; in Pennsylvania, *twenty-five* dollars per acre.

Does any one need to be told which state is able to pay and will pay the largest amount of revenue to the government? Is it not easy to see that, with the same policy in Virginia which has prevailed in Pennsylvania, that state would in a very few years be as populous, as wealthy, and as great a source of revenue, as her neighbor? And is it not to the interest of every free workingman, every tax-payer, that this should be brought about?

The Southern states, if we include Missouri and Kentucky, have an area of 851,508 square miles ; ·the free states have an area of only 612,597 square miles. The South has a milder climate, shorter winters, a far more fertile soil, immensely greater mineral wealth, more abundant natural water communications with the sea, than the North. Yet in 1850, by the census, the total value of the real and personal property of the free states was $1,161,081,000 *greater* than that of the real and personal property of the South, *including three millions of slaves.* But in 1860, according to the census of that year, the total value of real and personal property in the free states was $2,657,165,268 *greater* than that of the South. The wealth of , the free states, excluding the territories, was in 1860, in round numbers, nine thousand two hundred and eighty-seven millions ; that of the slave states, including Missouri, six thousand six hundred and thirty millions, also including the slaves !

Now if, by wise measures, by encouraging the mechanic arts, fostering free schools, developing mineral resources, and, in short, treating the South as we treated the Northwest, we can make it increase as rapidly, after the war, in free population, and in wealth, as the Northwest has, we may expect this difference to disappear in a very few years; we may expect the South to become as prosperous and as wealthy, in a few years, as the North is. In that case *it will contribute a revenue to the government greater than the whole North does at this time. That is to say, we can double our revenue without increasing our taxation, or we can raise the same revenue with half the taxes.*

But to do that we must do away with the wasteful and ruinous system of slave-labor which has made sterile the lands of the South, driven out her mechanics and artisans, made poor her people, and decreased her wealth. We cannot afford to waste anything; but Olmsted wrote to a Texan friend as the fruit of " a large class of observations :"

" The natural elements of wealth in the soil of Texas will have been more exhausted in ten years, and with them the rewards offered by Providence to labor will have been more lessened than without slavery would have been the case in two hundred. After two hundred years' occupation of similar soils by a free laboring community, I have seen no such evidence of exhaustion as in Texas I have after ten years of slavery."

TESTIMONY OF SLAVEHOLDERS.

In 1859 Charleston had not a single ship-carpenter. In 1859 Governor Wise, of Virginia, said to his people :

" Commerce has long ago spread her sails, and sailed away from you. You have not, as yet, dug more coal than enough to warm yourselves at your own hearths; you have set no tilt-hammer of Vulcan to strike blows worthy of gods in your own iron foundries; you have not yet spun more that coarse cotton enough, in the way of manufacture, to clothe your own slaves. *You have no commerce, no mining, no manufactures.* You have relied alone on the single power of agriculture, and *such agriculture !* Your sedge-patches outshine the sun. Your inattention to your only source of wealth has scared the very bosom of mother earth. Instead of having to feed cattle on a thousand hills, you have had to chase the stump-tailed deer through the sedge-patches to procure a tough beefsteak. The present condition of things has existed too long in Virginia."

Thomas Marshall, another slaveholder, said :

"Slavery is ruinous to the whites; it retards improvement, *roots out an industrious population, banishes the yeomanry of the country ; deprives the spinner, the weaver, the smith, the shoemaker, the carpenter, of employment and support.*"

In little more than ten years Wisconsin lands became worth on an average nine dollars and fifty-four cents per acre; but after two hundred and fifty years those of Virginia, with all her natural advantages, were worth but eight dollars and twenty-seven cents per acre. Virginia, free, might have had as rapid an increase as Massachusetts ; she would have had in 1850, that is to say, a population of 7,751,324 whites, instead of 894,800. Consider what would have been her wealth, with such an enormous population. Consider what would have been her ability, with her minerals, her water-power, her grain fields and her seacoast, to contribute to the national revenue.

If we want to lighten the burden of taxation, we must give the South the same opportunity for growth and increase which has made the West and Northwest so populous and rich in the last twenty-five years. But to do that, we must encourage free labor there—for it is the free workingman who makes the land rich—and the free man will not and cannot toil in competition with the slave.

THE WASTEFULNESS OF SLAVE LABOR.

The slave-labor system exhausts the soil, wastes its products, and contirbutes less—a very great deal less—to the national wealth, than the more skilful and intelligent free labor. The slave workman cannot be trusted with machinery ; he cannot be trusted with the best tools ; he must have—so the slave-holders themselves have said—the coarsest, rudest tools ; anything else he breaks. Now every workingman knows that with heavy, rough tools he cannot accomplish as much as another man can with light, well-made, handy tools. Every working man knows that it makes a world of difference what sort of a plough, what sort of an axe, what sort of a plane, what sort of a hammer he uses. He wants the best ; he knows that it pays him to have the best ; and he knows, too, that if he can make a machine saw, or plane, or mortice, or do anything else for him, that is so much gained—so much more money made in a given time. But the slave laborer cannot be trusted with any of these helps. Is it a wonder that with *a system which thus prevents the use of the best tools and machinery, the South is poor ?*

It is a fact, proved by the census, that *labor in Massachusetts is four times as productive as in South Carolina.* The average value of the product *per head* of the cotton factories of Massachusetts was in 1855, §725—ten times greater than the average value of the products of labor in South Carolina. The State of Massachusetts, with the help of skilled and industrious free labor, sent annually into the commerce of the world, *values greater than that of the entire cotton crop of the South !* Such is the enormous difference between slave labor and free labor.

Mr. Guthrie, in his report on the finances, in 1854-5, prepared a table from the census report, showing the average value of products per head in the different States. A comparison of some of the Free States with some of the Slave States, will show how much more productive is free labor than slave labor. In Massachusetts, with a bleak climate and a sterile soil, the average product per head of the population is valued at $166 00 ; in South Carolina but $56 91 ; in New York, $111 94 ; in Georgia, the Empire State of the South, $61 45 ; in Pennsylvania, $99 30 ; in Virginia, $59 42 ; in Ohio, $75 82 ; in Arkansas, $52 04 ; and in North Carolina, $49 38.

SLAVERY LOWERS THE VALUE OF LAND.

But this is not all; slave labor not only produces far less, and thus adds less to the taxable wealth of the community ; it at the same time wastes and ruins the substance of the country. It ruins the soil. The cotton planters were continually removing westward, with their slaves, to new lands ; and Olmstead reports that in Texas even, recently settled as it is, he already found the two curses of the planter—worn out and abandoned plantations and " poor whites." In North Carolina, six bushels of wheat to the acre is counted a fair crop. Compare Virginia and Pennsylvania, and we find, by the census report, that the actual crops per acre of corn were, in *Virginia eighteen*, and in *Pennsylvania thirty-six* bushels; of tobacco, in Virginia—whose speciality is tobacco—630 pounds per acre, in Pennsylvania 730 pounds. Under the slave-labor system of the South, according to Mr. Gregg, an accredited writer on the southern side, South Carolina had, before the war, one hundred and twenty-five thousand *white* persons "who ought to work and who do not, or who are so employed as to be wholly unproductive to the State."

Does anyone imagine that it is not the slave system, but the climate, which is to blame for this enormous and ruinous waste of labor and of the natural resources of the South? In Virginia, wherever, before the war, free labor got the upper hand, and slavery was driven out, there productions were at once largely increased. The Charleston *Standard* remarked, in 1857, "The Virginia journalists have frequently borne witness to the fact, that in many districts where large estates have been divided and sold to small farmers, the land is turning off from three to six times as much produce as it did a few years ago." In Cahill, Mason, Brooke, and Tyler counties, Virginia, which had, before the war, a free laboring population, with slaves but one in fifteen to the freemen, but no advantages of towns in or near them, land was worth, in 1855, $7 75 per acre. In Southampton, Surrey, James Town, and New Kent counties, in the same state, where the slave population was as 1 to 2, the *land was worth but half as much*, $4 50 per acre. In Fairfax county the slave population was much reduced within the last twenty-five years; free laboring men took the places of the slave laborers; and the County Commissioners reported officially:

"In appearance, the county is so changed, in many parts, that a traveller, who passed over it ten years ago, would not now recognize it. Thousands and thousands of acres had been cultivated in Tobacco, by the former proprietors, would not pay the cost, and were abandoned as worthless, and became covered with a wilderness of pines. These lands have been purchased by *northern emigrants ;* the large tracts divided and subdivided, and cleared of pines ; and neat farm-houses and barns, with smiling fields of grain and grass, in the season, salute the delighted gaze of the beholder. Ten years ago, it was a mooted question whether Fairfax lands could be made productive ; and, if so, would they pay the cost ? This problem has been satisfactorily solved by many, and, in consequence of the above altered state of things, *school-houses and churches have doubled in number.*"

That is to say, slavery makes a rich country poor, free labor makes a poor country rich ; slave labor—improvident, wasteful, unskillful—rots out the heart of the land, and, finally, leaves the soil when it can no longer make a living from it: free labor comes in, and, in ten years, restores the soil, and works it at so great a profit that the face of the country is changed, and " churches and schools are doubled." *But mark ! until slave labor is driven out, free labor will not come in.* The two systems cannot work together. Which, then, shall we protect— the slavemaster, who impoverishes the country, or the free laborer who enriches it ?

The Wheeling *Intelligencer,* then published in a slave state, spoke out on this question, some ten years ago, in the following words :

" The present great and pressing want of our state, like that of the whole United States, is cultivation and improvement, not enlargement and annexation, and the obvious and the only mode of a rapid growth of our state or city is such a change of public policy as shall invite to our aid and co operation our Caucasian cousins, the intelligent, moral, and industrious artizans, mechanics, miners, manufacturers, and commercial men of Europe and the northern states, to share our taxation, develop our resources, and make ours a *white man's country,* with all the energy, education, love of order, of freedom, and of order characteristic of the Anglo-Saxon race. The history of the world, and especially of the States of this Union, shows most conclusively that *public prosperity bears an almost mathematical proportion to the degree of freedom enjoyed by all the inhabitants of the state.* Men will always work better for the cash than for the lash. The free laborer will produce and save as much, and consume and waste as little as he can. The slave, on the contrary, will produce and save as little, and consume and waste as much as possible. Hence states and counties filled with the former class must necessarily flourish and increase in population, arts, manufactures, wealth, and education, because they are animated and incited by all the vigor of the will ; while states filled with the latter class must exhibit comparative stagnation, because it is the universal law of nature that force and fear end in ruin and decay."

5

EFFECTS OF FREE AND SLAVE LABOR CONTRASTED.

In the newly settled free states we find villages, towns, churches, schools, and other conveniences of civilization springing up in the immediate track of the settlers; in the slave states, on the contrary, these are to a great extent lacking. The free workingman of Iowa, or Minnesota, may count upon being able to send his children to good schools, to attend church with his family, to enjoy the profits of a sale in an adjacent village for all the "small truck" of his farm, if he is a farmer; or if he is a mechanic, to obtain employment, through the gathering of the population in villages and towns, to afford him a comfortable living. In the slave states, on the contrary, even in the oldest settled of them, towns and villages are few and far apart; the small farmer can find no sale for his chickens, eggs, vegetables or fruits; the free mechanic is restricted to the few cities where alone he can find employment; all inducements to any methods of mechanical labor, or of farming, not practised in cities or upon great slave plantations, are lacking.

So few are the towns, even in the long settled states of Georgia and South Carolina, that a large part of the railroad stations are numbered—as station 1, station 2, station 14; and where, as at Millen, and other points, a name is given, there is, in most cases, no town or village, but only a dépôt for cotton.

SLAVERY LEAVES NO CHANCE FOR SMALL FARMERS.

Of course, in such a country, with such a state of affairs, the small farmer, and the country carpenter, blacksmith, wheelwright, &c., have no chance to live. The small farmer, with us in the free states, carries his chickens, eggs, feathers, turkeys, pigs, apples, and other minor produce to the "store," in the next village, and with this produce often clothes his family, and keeps up the supply of tea, coffee and sugar, while the staple of his farm, his grain or cattle, go to pay the cost of labor, and other expenses, and to form the balance of profit, which laid by, makes him yearly a more comfortable and independent man. But in the slave states this small farmer is surrounded by great plantations; no town or village is near him where he can sell the profitable "small truck;" he must neglect this important source of profit for the man of few acres; he toils away in the cotton field, and *his wife toils with him;* and they are no better off at the year's end than at the beginning.

Moreover, he does not enjoy the intellectual benefit of a weekly visit to a town or village; his children have no school provided for them; he and his wife cannot often go to church. He is deprived, too, of the numberless conveniences which the numerous villages and towns, even in the most recently settled free states, afford to the farmer there. If he needs the services of a carpenter, or tailor, or blacksmith, or wagon maker, of any mechanic, the farmer of the slave states must either set out on a long journey over bad roads, for fifty or sixty miles—or he must do without. In South Carolina, to this day, the country people are obliged, in this way, to make their own rude, heavy, inconvenient wagons, often without a tire on the wheels, which are not unfrequently of solid wood. They must make their own ill-fitting harness; they must build their own rude cabins; no mason, or plasterer, or carpenter, or skilled mechanic can be found to help them; on the rich plantations such mechanics are found—*but they are slaves.*

There is thus, in the condition of society which is created by the slave labor system, *no room, and no encouragement for the free mechanic and the small farmer,* who make up the bulk of our population in the free states, and whose industry, and thrift and intelligence make the country prosperous and happy.

Does any one ask why this is so? Why has slavery this singular and disastrous effect? Because the wealthy own slaves, and "do not need the services of the free workingmen," to quote once more the words of Marion. The rich planter living upon his estate, owns his slave mechanics, goes North or to Europe when he wants to amuse himself, and has no interest in the social advancement of the county in which he happens to be settled. *What should he care for schools? his children have tutors at home, or go to northern colleges.* Why should he seek to form or elevate society around him? When he wants "company" he goes to Charleston, or Savannah, or Mobile, or New Orleans, or New York. Why should he buy the small farmer's "truck"? *His own slaves raise all he wants.* Why should he employ free mechanics? He prefers to *buy* a carpenter and sell him again when the work is done. Moreover, he would not help to support the village store, if there was one—for *he buys his supplies at wholesale in the great city.* He does not need the village tailor, for his clothes are made in New York. His wife does not not employ the village milliner, for she gets her dresses from New Orleans, or New York, or Paris.

In short, the planter has no interest in the county where he happens to own soil, except to raise as much cotton off the land as possible; he spends the proceeds away from home.

WHY THE SLAVE STATES LACK CAPITAL.

But with this, there has been a singular complaint amongst the planters, which meets one in almost every essay printed by DeBow; a complaint of a lack of capital. "The south needs capital" was the constant cry. "Our tanneries will not succeed, because of our limited capital," says a writer on the resources of Georgia. "For the last twenty years, floating capital, to the amount of $500,000 per annum has left Charleston, and gone out of the state" complained Governor Hammond, in a famous essay on Southern Industry. "Ninety millions of capital," he says in another place, "has been drained out of South Carolina in twenty years;" and another writer, urging the establishment of manufactories in the south, admits that "we have not the capital to spare." *We do not hear such complaints in the free states.* Our workmen are not idle, our mines are not undeveloped, our manufactories are not stopped for want of capital.

But they would be, if the manufacturer—or mine owner—had not only to buy his machinery, *but also his workmen.* No company, however wealthy, could afford to run a mill in Lowell, or work a coal mine in Pennsylvania, or keep up a furnace in Pittsburgh, if it had to provide means, not only to pay for its machinery but to buy also its working men and women. All the industry of the free states would come to a stand still if this system should suddenly be forced upon us. No wonder the manufacturing industry of the South was never set going "for lack of capital."

But this same mischief has injured the South in other ways. Look, for instance, at this: Take two men, both farmers; let one remove to Texas, the other to Iowa; let each have his land purchased; and have five thousand dollars over. Each needs a carpenter to build a comfortable house for him. The Iowan gives notice in the newspapers—which are glad to print such intelligence—that carpenters can get higher wages in his neighborhood than farther East; and he readily gets the services of an enterprising young mechanic. But the Texan? He must *buy his carpenter;* he must pay probably two thousand dollars for the man. He has but three thousand left—the Iowan has spent only the wages of a carpenter while he needed him.

That done, each requires three laborers to clear and cultivate the new land. The Iowan advertises, offers good wages, and gets his men without trouble; *the Texan must pay out his remaining three thousand dollars for three slaves.* He has now all his money invested—the Iowan, however, has yet the greater part of his in hand. He is able to purchase the best implements —but the Texan must manage without or run in debt. He is able to contribute to the building of a school and church; but the Texan, in the first place, has no money left for such purposes; and in the next place, the children of his slaves must not be educated. *Therefore, his own children have no school or church.* The Iowan, having still say two thousand dollars in hand, may set up a friend, in a mill, or a store—and both will be supported by the laboring population which he has gathered about him, who are earning wages and will purchase clothing and provisions. But the Texan has no money to loan for such enterprises; and if he had, they could not succeed, for his slaves have no wages to spend, and he gets his supplies at wholesale, from his factor in New Orleans or Shreveport.

Let any one, farmer or laboring man, answer, who is the most comfortable, whose children have the best chance to grow up intelligent, who has the most money at command, the Texan slave owner, or the Iowan farmer? who builds up around him the most quickly, a thriving community? who gives employment to free mechanics? whose skill and capital is most productive of wealth and progress, and happiness, to the neighborhood?

We see by this instance, how it is that in the South they always " lacked capital." The Texan emptied his purse before he got fairly started; the Iowan had money in hand when his farm was thoroughly furnished. The Texan was condemned by the slave system to live in solitude—the Iowan at once, and necessarily, gathered a little company about him, of working-men, and mechanics, and their families, and if he selected his farm wisely, he saw within a year a little village spring up near him, with its schools, church, stores, and proper supply of me-chanics of different kinds.

Mechanics and laboring men, remember, that the slave sys-tem leaves no room for you! It shuts you out! The Southern planter does not need you; he cannot bear your independent ways; he " buys a carpenter when he wants one." He and his fellow planters have, for half a century, shut up, against you and your families, the finest part of the Union ; *while slavery lasts you can gain no foothold there, for every slaveholder is your enemy ;* your children can have no schools there; you can have none of the conveniences of life; you cannot even get em-ployment. But do away with the slave system, make all labor free, take away from the rich planter his fatal monopoly, let every man who works be paid wages according to his ability, and let every employer pay just wages to his workmen, and you can safely go to the South, and take with you the society, the schools, the churches, the frequent villages and towns, all the conveniences of civilization, which the slave labor system has not.

Slavery is the free workingman's worst enemy; let this truth be spread abroad amongst you, free workingmen of the North and South ! Then, for your own sakes, and for the sake of your children, *whom you do not wish to grow up in the overcrowded North*, let slavery die. In the South, if slavery is abolished, *the wages of mechanics and laboring men must for many years to come be very high.* That whole vast region is almost with-out skilled labor; free mechanics have been driven from it. *A region greater than all the free states, as healthful, with a finer climate, more abundant mineral resources, cheaper lands and a richer soil, lies open before you and your families.* You have only to possess it, and with your skill and energy subdue it.

Then you will not feel the hard struggle which severe climate, and tenement houses, and lack of employment, and the oppression caused by an overcrowded labor market, subjected you to in the North. *But you can never enter that land of ease and plenty; without first striking down your fatal enemy, slavery !*